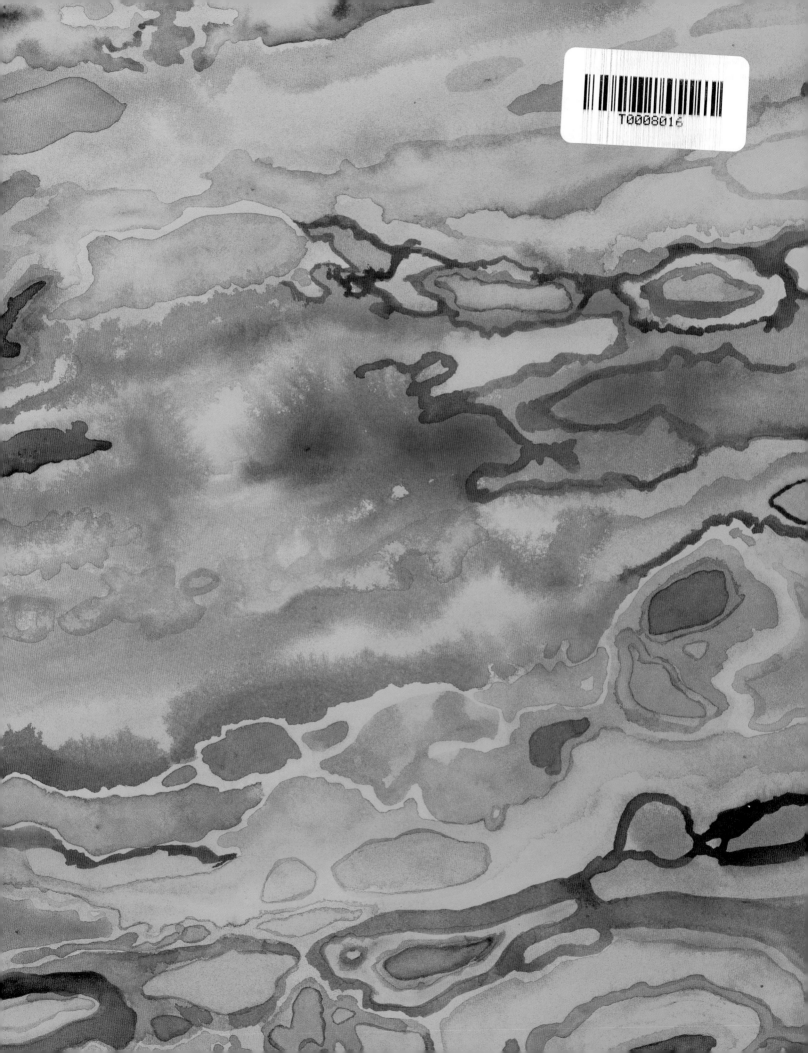

A Shell Is Cozy

Dianna Hutts Aston   Sylvia Long

To Candy and Mark Shelts, Candi Rodocker Hill,
the Brandon family, Lisa King, and my island friends
in Port Aransas, Texas; and to Sylvia Long, Victoria Rock,
Sara Gillingham, and the entire team at Chronicle Books.
And special thanks to Tina Petway, associate curator,
The Houston Museum of Natural Science, for her expertise,
and to research assistant Katie McCrillis. —D. H. A.

For Sophie and H-Dog,
remembering perfect days at the beach,
searching for agates and colorful empty shells. —S. L.

Library of Congress Cataloging-in-Publication Data available.

ISBN 978-1-7972-1247-0

Manufactured in China.

Design by Sara Gillingham Studio.
Hand lettered by Anne Robin and Sylvia Long.
The illustrations in this book were rendered in ink and watercolor.

10 9 8 7 6 5 4 3 2 1

Chronicle books and gifts are available at special quantity
discounts to corporations, professional associations, literacy programs,
and other organizations. For details and discount information,
please contact our premiums department at
corporatesales@chroniclebooks.com or at 1-800-759-0190.

Chronicle Books LLC
680 Second Street
San Francisco, California 94107

Chronicle Books—we see things differently.
Become part of our community at www.chroniclekids.com.

A Shell Is Cozy

Dianna Hutts Aston Sylvia Long

chronicle books · san francisco

Common warrener

A shell is cozy...

a cozy, bony shelter that
keeps the soft, delicate parts
of the shelled animal
safely tucked inside.

Royal thorny
oyster

A shell

Mollusks are a group of
shelled animals that include bivalves,
tusk shells, and gastropods.

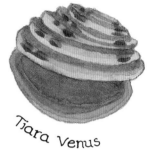

Tiara Venus

A bivalve has two shells
held together by a gummy hinge.
It can open and close like a door.

Purple clam

Royal cloak scallop

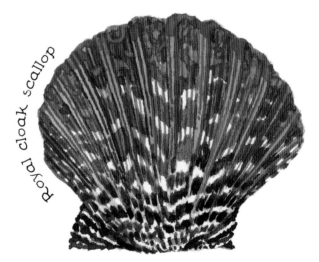

A tusk shell, sometimes called an elephant's tusk shell
or elephant's tooth shell, has two openings.
Sticky tentacles poke out from the larger end to
pick up and carry food particles to its mouth.

Common tusk

Green tusk

is showy.

Candy cane snail

Wavy turban snail

Most gastropods have only one opening with a lid-like door—
called an operculum—that can be as thin as a fingernail.
This door quickly closes when the animal is in danger.

Painted snails

Green turban

A shell is hatched...

Queen conch laying eggs

Most mollusks begin life as eggs nestled in soil, gently swaying on eelgrass, snuggled up in egg capsules, or coiled in long strands.

The coiled egg strands of the queen conch may contain as many as half a million eggs.

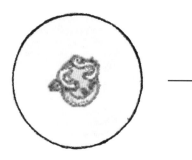 —  —

In 3–5 days, the eggs hatch into microscopic larvae.

8–10 days later, each larva develops 6 lobes that help it swim.

21–40 days after hatching, each larva goes through metamorphosis to become a tiny conch (1–2 millimetres).

It takes 3–5 years for a queen conch to reach adult size— 12 inches (30.5 centimetres).

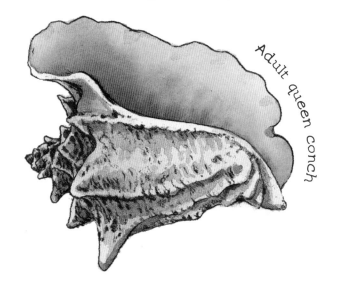
Adult queen conch

and protective

Mollusks have a fleshlike layer, called a mantle,
that secretes calcium carbonate—a shell-building liquid
that hardens upon contact with air or water.
With each coating, the shell grows larger.

The mantle also protects the animal's soft organs.

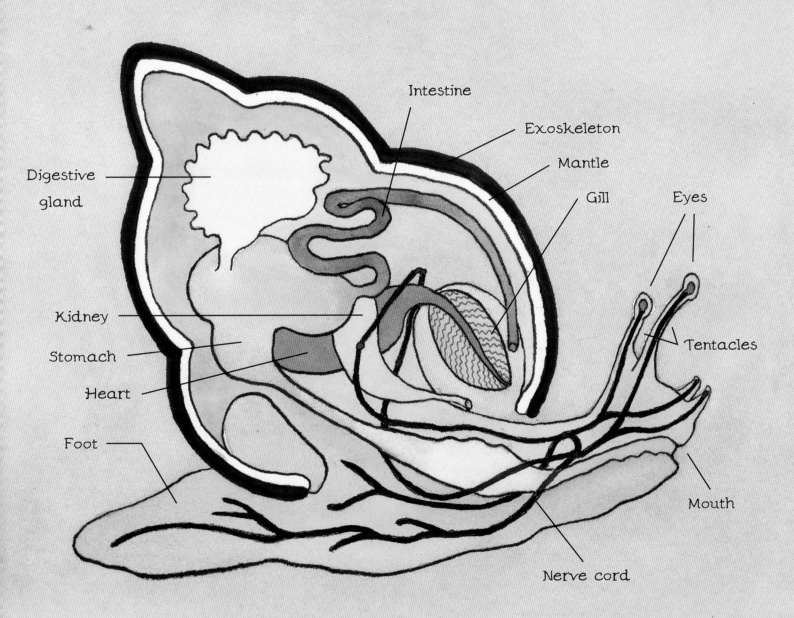

Intestine

Exoskeleton

Mantle

Gill

Eyes

Digestive
gland

Tentacles

Kidney

Stomach

Heart

Foot

Mouth

Nerve cord

partridge tun

A shell is everywhere.

Shells can be found
in fresh water,
slip-sliding through mud
and clinging to stones;

in salt water,
scurrying through
the sand and sea
and hiding in
coral reefs; and . . .

Giant clam

Triton's trumpet

on land,
climbing into treetops,

Candy cane snails

High above the ground,
a shell is safe from
hungry predators below.

dwelling deep inside caves, and hiding from the desert sun.

Domed
land snail

In lightless caves deep beneath the earth's surface,
the domed land snail's shell is translucent, or see-through.

In deserts, where the temperature is extremely high,
shells are often white, the color that best reflects sunlight.

Phoenix
talussnail

A shell is hungry

Zebra moon snail

Some mollusks are carnivores that feed on worms, jellyfish, and even other mollusks. Many have a radula, a floss-like "tongue" with thousands of razor-sharp teeth. With its radula, the animal can saw through another shell to feed on the juicy insides.

Marbled cone snail

A marbled cone snail's siphon emerges to locate prey by scent. Then it spears its victim with a venomous, harpoon-like radula, instantly paralyzing it.

Some are filter feeders. Animals like clams, scallops,
and mussels draw water into their gills with vacuum-like siphons
and trap tiny food particles such as algae and plankton.

Coquina clams

Brown-lipped snail

Some are herbivores
whose diets include fruits,
vegetables, and algae.

Garden snail

Roman snail

White-lipped snail

A shell is athletic.

Sea scallops "clap" their shells together to swim swiftly away from meal-chasing carnivores like crabs and sea stars.

Sea scallops

Bladder snail

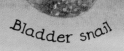

Great pond snail

Assassin snail

Some water snails can hang upside
down from the water's surface,
clinging to it with gluey mucus.

Queen conch

With its talon-like operculum and
muscular foot, the queen conch digs
into the sand, then flips and tumbles
like a gymnast to escape predators.

Venus comb

A shell is spiny...

Spines protect it
from predators like
stingrays and fish.

Babylon snail

smooth...

Dark-spotted auger

Purple olive

Assassin snail

Plough

A smooth, narrow shell
slips into the sand or mud
as easily as water passes
through a hose.

Angel wing clam

sharp...

With the toothy ridges of its shell,
the angel wing clam drills into rocks,
wood, or mud to make its home.
Only its straw-like siphon extends
beyond the entrance,
so it can feed on tiny organisms.

and even hairy!

Cobwebs and bits of dirt
cling to the short, stiff hairs on
the shell of the velvet wedge
to help camouflage it.

Velvet wedges

A shell is artistic.

Inspired by a famous Renaissance painting of the Roman goddess Venus rising from the sea on a scallop shell, fashion designer Christian Dior created a ball gown called the Venus that had silvery netting that looked like sea-foam and a train made of scallop shell-shaped fabric.

Christian Dior Venus dress, 1949

Contemporary jazz musician Steve Turre plays the same kind of shell instrument in his recordings as his Aztec ancestors did when they trumpete to mark time, make announcement or call for battle to begin.

Broken glass, tile, rocks, and about 10,000 seashells adorn the Watts Towers, a National Historic Landmark constructed by Italian immigrant Simon Rodia in the early twentieth century.

A shell is enormous...

The largest bivalve is the giant clam.
Giant clams can grow to more than
4 feet (1.2 metres) in length and can weigh
more than 400 pounds (180 kilograms)—
as much as a lion! Because of their size,
they have been used as small bathtubs,
birdbaths, baptismal fonts, and fountains.

Giant clam

Dwarf shell

and
microscopic.

The dwarf shell holds the
world record as the tiniest shell,
with a diameter of 0.028 inches
(0.7 millimetres). It is so small
that researchers need a microscope
to study it. However, scientists
continue to search for shells
that are even smaller.

A shell is treasured . . .

Shells were among the earliest forms of currency,
or money. People traded shells for necessities like
food, land, weapons, and canoes.

Images of shells can be found on coins all around the world.

Sumerian shell money

Yurok dentalium
shell money

New Guinea
giant clam
money shell

BRONZE SHELL COINS

Roman (cockle)

Greek (scallop)

Chinese
(cowrie)

COINS DEPICTING SHELLS

Bahamian

ONE DOLLAR

(conch)

Australian

AUSTRALIAN ABALONE SHELL

(abalone)

When a bit of shell or a tiny
animal is trapped inside a
shell, it can become a pearl
as small as a pea or as
large as a golf ball . . .
and possibly pink!

Freshwater
oyster pearl

VANUATU COINS

Triton's trumpet

VATU

Nautilus

MILLENNIUM 2000

750 VATU

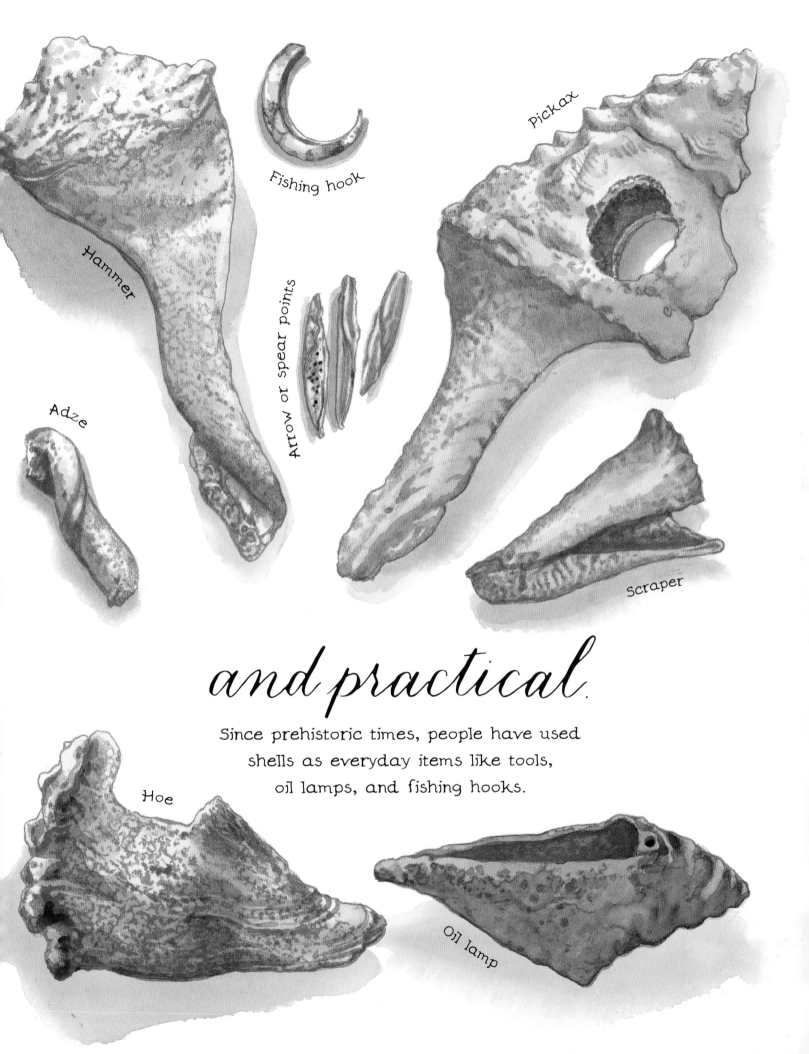

Fishing hook

Pickax

Hammer

Arrow or spear points

Adze

Scraper

and practical.

Since prehistoric times, people have used
shells as everyday items like tools,
oil lamps, and fishing hooks.

Hoe

Oil lamp

When a mollusk has finished its life —

roaming the ocean,
tumbling through rivers,
creeping across deserts—
it leaves its empty shell behind
to become a nursery for fish eggs,
a hiding place for an octopus,
or a hermit crab's new home.

Then a shell
is once again . . .

Hermit crab

cozy!

Green turban

Coquina clam

Dark-spotted auger

Tiara Venus

Green tusk

Venus comb

Purple olive

Partridge tun

Velvet wedge

Brown-lipped snail

Angel wing clam

Marbled cone snail

Babylon snail

Dwarf shell

Garden snail

Candy cane snail

Bladder snail

Royal cloak scallop

Common warrener

White-lipped snail

Phoenix talussnail

Sea scallop

Abalone

Queen conch

Assassin snail

Triton's trumpet

Painted snail

Common tusk

Wavy turban snail

Zebra moon snail

Domed land snail

Purple clam

Royal thorny oyster

Great pond snail

Giant clam

Roman snail

Plough snail

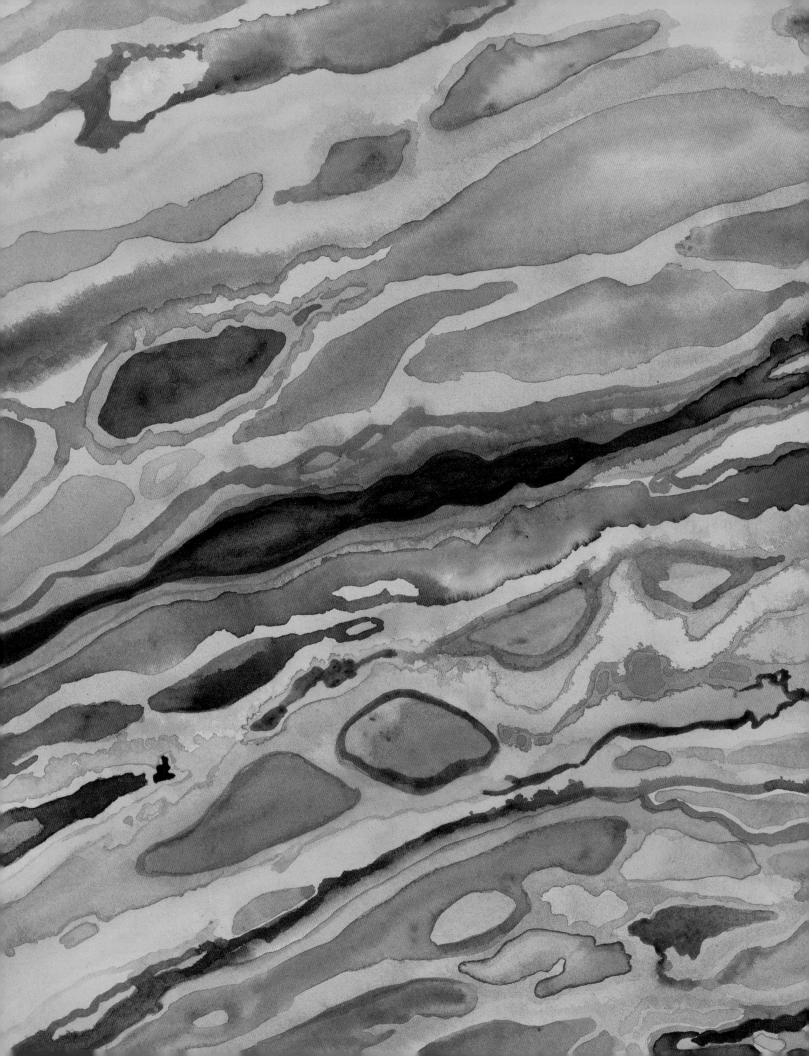